CONTINENTS

Asia

Leila Merrell Foster

Heinemann
LIBRARY

www.heinemann.co.uk/library
Visit our website to find out more information about Heinemann Library books.

To order:

☎ Phone ++44 (0)1865 888066

📄 Send a fax to ++44 (0)1865 314091

💻 Visit the Heinemann Bookshop at www.heinemann.co.uk/library to browse our catalogue and order online.

First published in Great Britain by Heinemann Library, Halley Court, Jordan Hill, Oxford OX2 8EJ, a division of Reed Educational and Professional Publishing Ltd. Heinemann is a registered trademark of Reed Educational and Professional Publishing Ltd.

OXFORD MELBOURNE AUCKLAND JOHANNESBURG BLANTYRE GABORONE IBADAN PORTSMOUTH NH (USA) CHICAGO

Designed by Depke Design
Originated by Dot Gradations
Printed by South China Printing in Hong Kong, China

06 05 04 03 02
10 9 8 7 6 5 4 3 2 1
ISBN 0 431 15791 X

British Library Cataloguing in Publication Data
  Foster, Leila Merrell
  Asia. – (Continents)
  1.Asia – Juvenile literature
  I.Title
  915

Acknowledgements
The publishers are grateful to the following for permission to reproduce copyright material:
Tony Stone/Mike Surowiak, p. 4; Bruce Coleman, Inc./L. Veisman, p. 7; Bruce Coleman, Inc./J. Montgomery, p. 8; Bruce Coleman, Inc./Burnett H. Moody, p. 11; Earth Scenes/Robert Kloepper, p. 12; Tony Stone/Hugh Sitton, p. 15; Bruce Coleman, Inc./Lynn M. Stone, p. 16; Bruce Coleman, Inc./K&K Ammann, p. 17; Tony Stone/Mickey Gibson, p. 18; Bruce Coleman, Inc./M. Freeman, p. 19; Tony Stone/D.E. Cox, p. 21; Tony Stone/Orion Press, p. 22; Bruce Coleman, Inc./Carolos V. Causo, p. 25; Tony Stone/Keren Su, p. 26; Corbis/Glen Allison, p. 27; Tony Stone/Chris Haigh, p. 28.

Cover photo reproduced with permission of Science Photo Library/Worldsat International and J. Knighton.

Our thanks to Jane Bingham for her assistance in the preparation of this book.

Every effort has been made to contact copyright holders of any material reproduced in this book. Any omissions will be rectified in subsequent printings if notice is given to the Publisher.

Contents

Some words are shown in bold, **like this**.
You can find out what they mean by looking in the glossary.

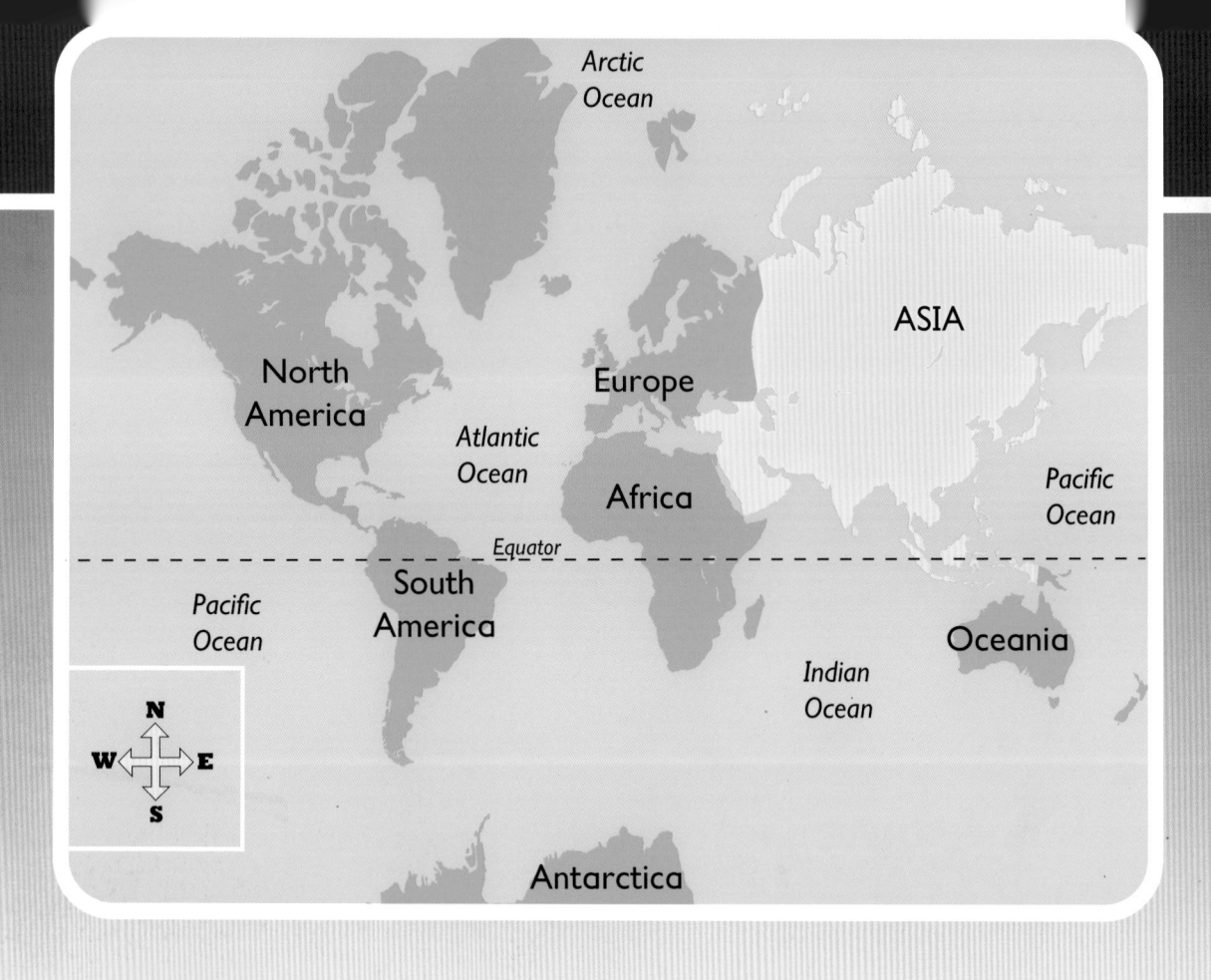

A continent is a vast mass of land that covers part of the Earth's surface. There are seven continents in the world, and Asia is the largest. To the west, Asia is connected to the continent of Europe. In the north, Asia stretches into the icy Arctic Ocean. In the south, it is crossed by the **equator**.

The island of Hong Kong, China

The continent of Asia lies between the Mediterranean Sea to the west and the Pacific Ocean to the east. The countries along the Pacific coast – China, Korea and Japan – are known as the Far East. The lands around the Mediterranean Sea – Turkey, Syria and Israel – are part of a **region** called the Middle East.

Weather

Frozen land in northern Russia

The countries of Asia have many different **climates**. In northern Russia, beyond the **Arctic Circle**, the land stays frozen all the year round. Further south, there are dry, windswept grasslands, with very cold winters. In central Asia, there are vast deserts, where almost no rain falls.

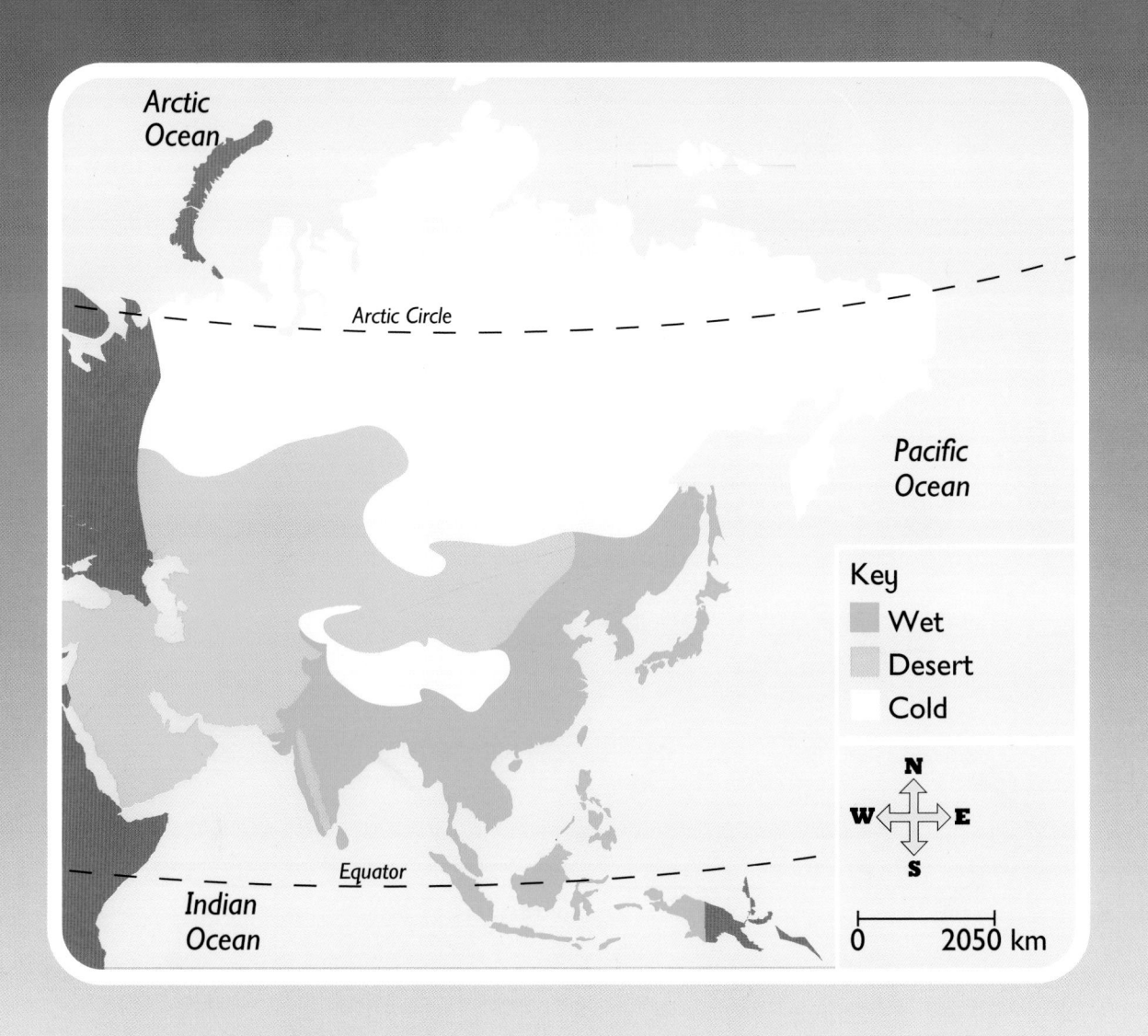

In the south of the continent, around the **equator**, the weather is very hot and **humid**. Large areas of South Asia are covered in steamy **rainforests**, where it rains every day. In the lands around the Mediterranean Sea, it is much drier, and the weather is warm and sunny all the year round.

Mount Everest, Nepal

The continent of Asia is crossed by many high mountain **ranges**. There are also large areas of high, rocky land known as plateaus. The Tibetan plateau in southern China is higher than most mountains in Europe or the USA. The Kunlun, Karakoram and Himalayan mountains all rise from this plateau.

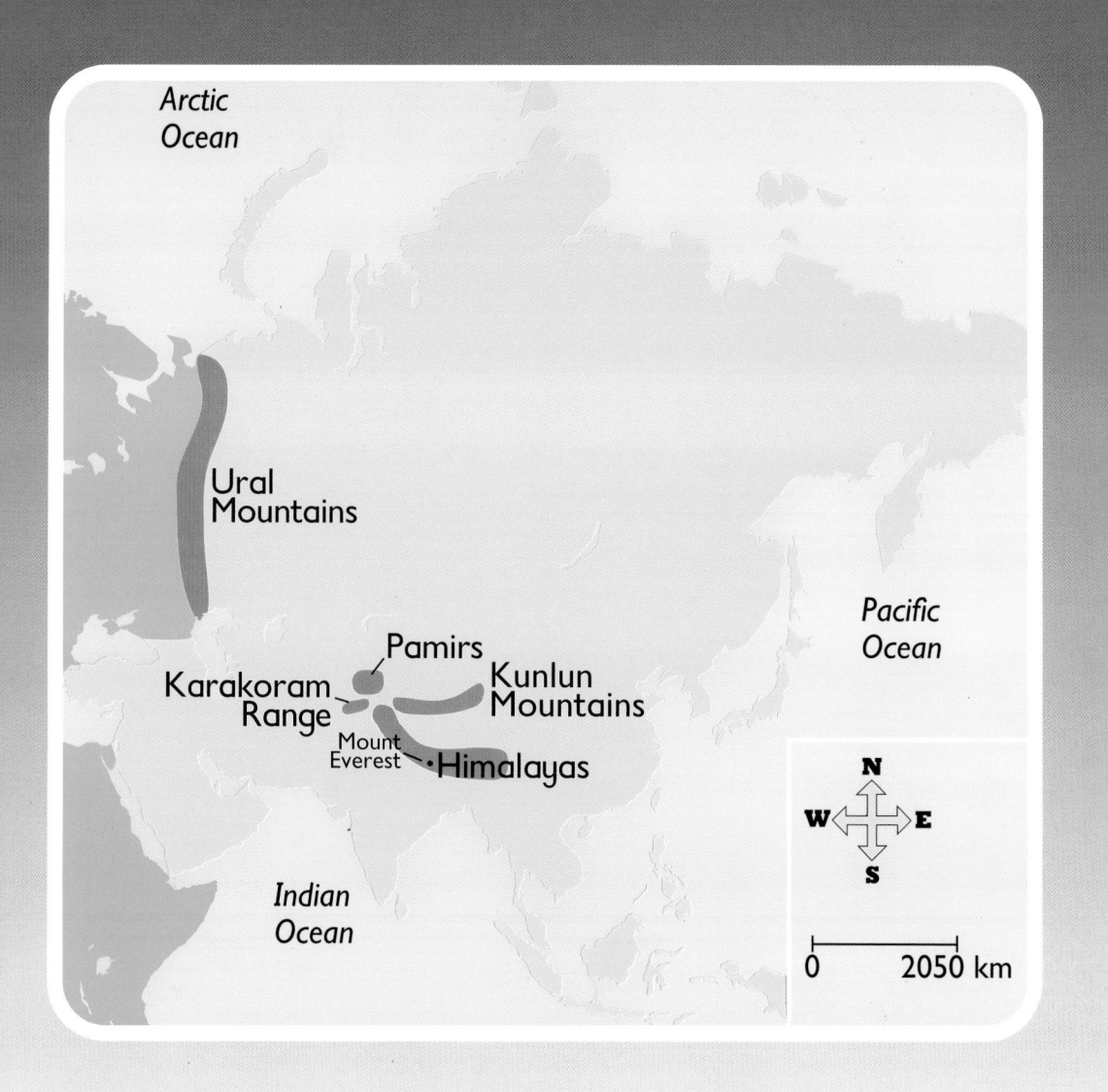

The Himalayan mountain range runs along the **border** of China and Nepal, and also passes through India and Bhutan. The highest point in the Himalayas is Mount Everest – the world's tallest mountain. Sir Edmund Hillary from New Zealand and Tenzing Norgay from Nepal reached the top of Everest in 1953.

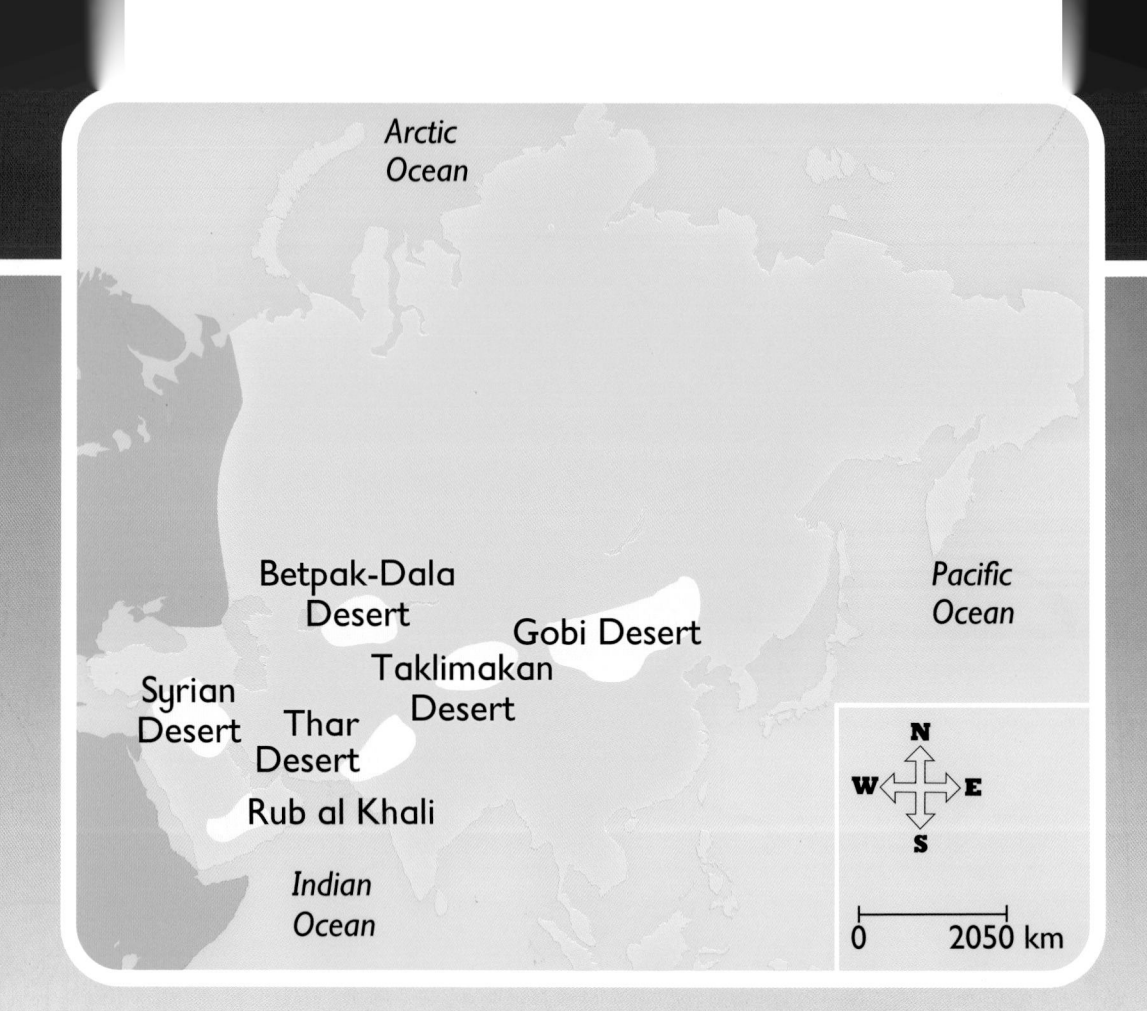

Large parts of central Asia are covered by desert. The Gobi Desert in China is bare and rocky, scorching hot in summer and freezing cold in winter. For hundreds of years, people called Mongols have lived in the Gobi Desert. They live in circular tents, called yurts, and keep moving from place to place.

Drilling for oil in Saudi Arabia

In the 1930s, oil was discovered beneath the sandy deserts of Saudi Arabia, in southwest Asia. People set up oil rigs in the desert to drill for oil and bring it to the surface. The oil is pumped through pipelines to ports on the coast. Then it is sent in large ships, called oil tankers, to countries all over the world.

Chang River, China

The Chang (or Yangtze) River is the third largest river in the world. It flows through China for 6380 kilometres. People have built huge dams on the Chang. As water rushes through these dams, it creates energy, which is turned into electricity. This kind of power is called hydroelectricity.

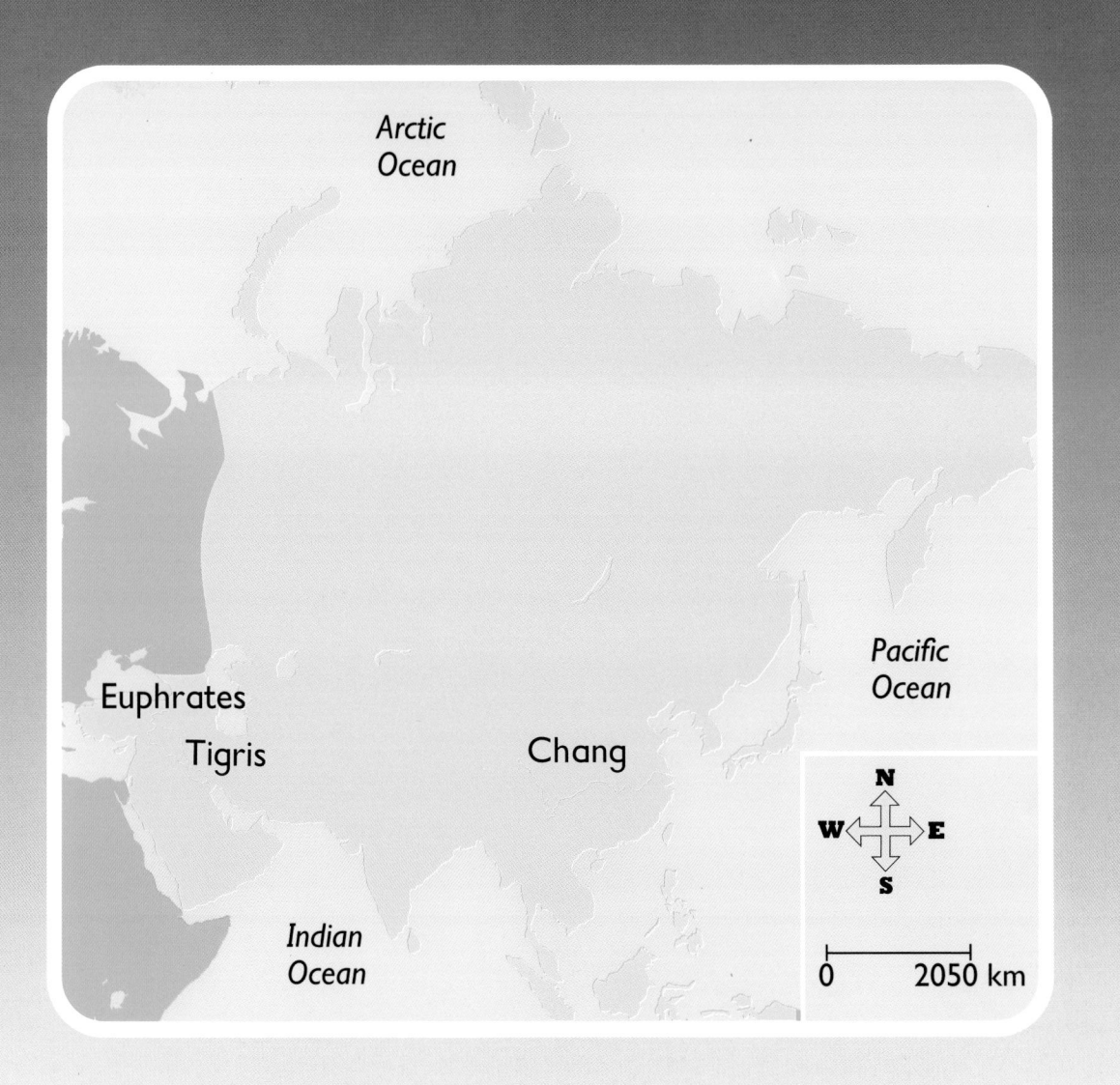

The world's first cities were built by people living near the Tigris and Euphrates rivers. The land between these rivers was very **fertile** so farmers could grow lots of crops. They sailed their boats on the rivers and traded goods with other people. The farmers became very rich and built splendid cities.

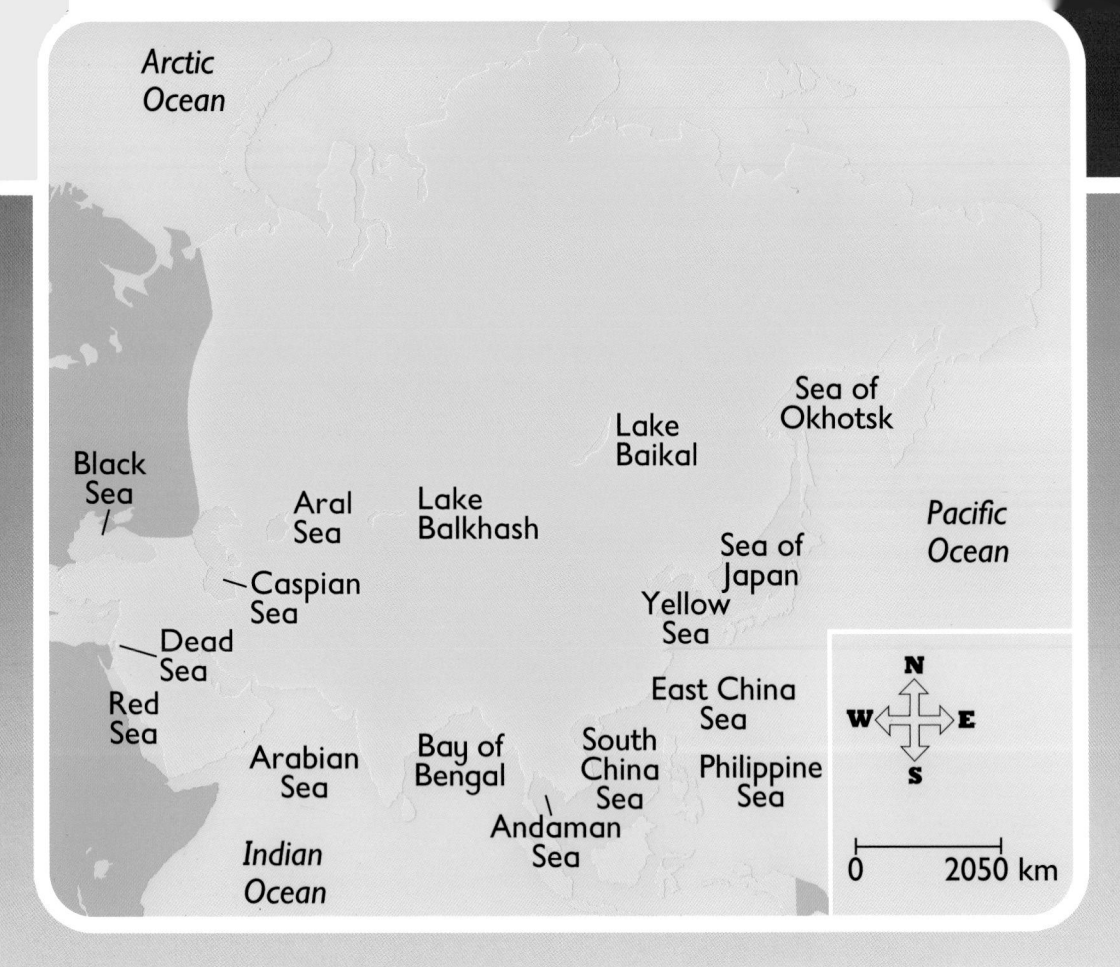

Asia has many large lakes. The largest of these is the Caspian Sea. Although it is called a sea, the Caspian is really the world's biggest **saltwater** lake. Fish called sturgeon swim in the Caspian Sea. The sturgeon's eggs are made into caviar, a very expensive fish paste.

Dead Sea, Israel

Like the Caspian Sea, the Dead Sea is really a lake. It is the lowest lake on Earth. It lies partly in Israel and partly in Jordan. The River Jordan runs into the Dead Sea but no river leaves it. There is so much salt in the water of the Dead Sea that people can float in it very easily.

Giant panda, China

The giant panda lives in the forests of southwest China. It feeds almost entirely on bamboo shoots. Giant pandas are in danger of becoming **extinct** and fewer than 1000 still live in the wild. The Chinese government has set aside special areas of forest where giant pandas can live safely.

Orangutan, Borneo

The orangutan is also very rare. This giant ape lives in swampy **rainforests** on the islands of Borneo and Sumatra. Orangutans used to live on the **mainland** of Southeast Asia, but they were hunted by humans. Now people are trying to protect the rainforests and the amazing creatures that live there.

Rice paddies, Indonesia

Farmers grow rice all over southern Asia. They plant the rice in flooded fields called rice paddies. Asian farmers grow most of the world's rice, rubber, cotton and tea. The islands of Southeast Asia are famous for their spices, such as nutmeg, pepper and cloves.

Bamboo plants in Indonesia

Bamboo grows in the forests of China and Southeast Asia. Although the bamboo plant grows as tall as a tree, it is actually a very fast growing grass. People use the woody bamboo stems to make houses, fishing poles and rafts. Some bamboo is made into furniture, which is then **exported** to other countries.

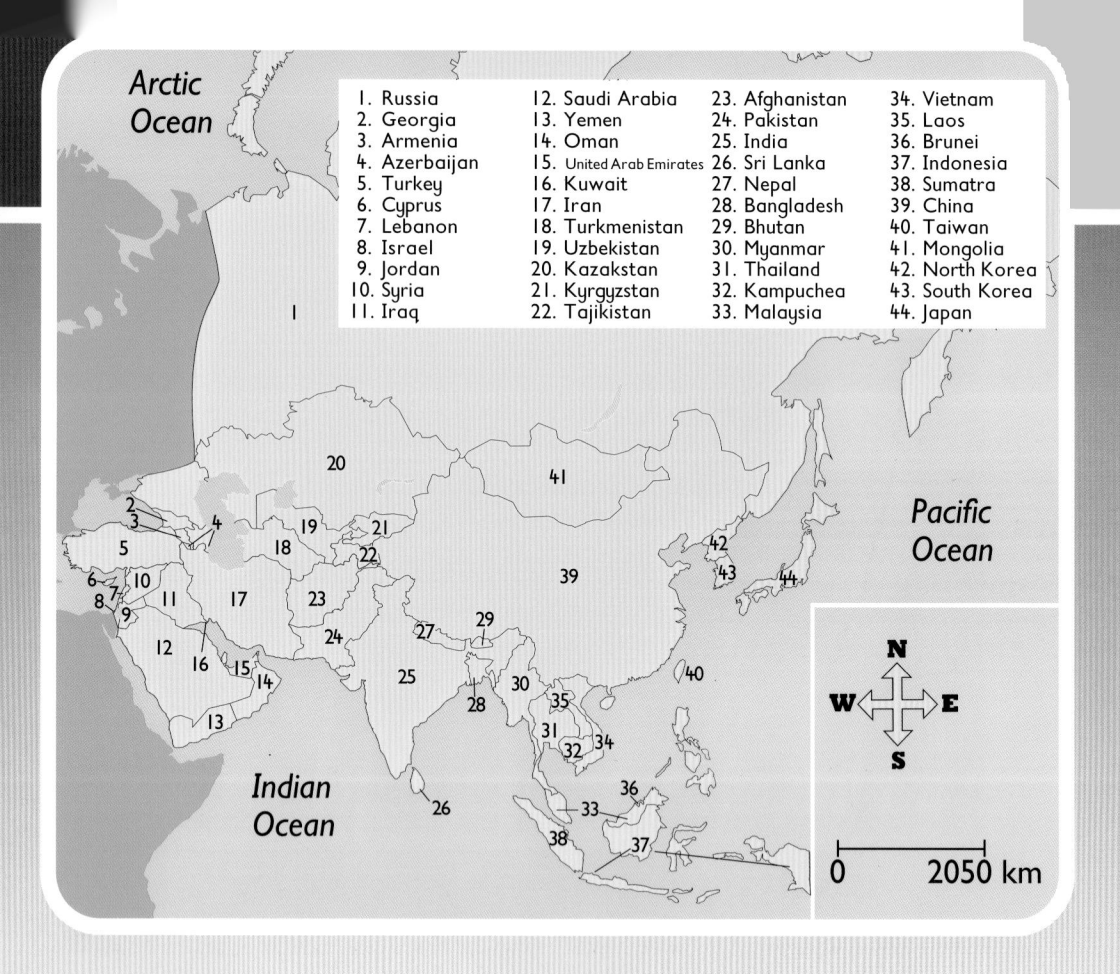

Arctic Ocean

1. Russia	12. Saudi Arabia	23. Afghanistan	34. Vietnam
2. Georgia	13. Yemen	24. Pakistan	35. Laos
3. Armenia	14. Oman	25. India	36. Brunei
4. Azerbaijan	15. United Arab Emirates	26. Sri Lanka	37. Indonesia
5. Turkey	16. Kuwait	27. Nepal	38. Sumatra
6. Cyprus	17. Iran	28. Bangladesh	39. China
7. Lebanon	18. Turkmenistan	29. Bhutan	40. Taiwan
8. Israel	19. Uzbekistan	30. Myanmar	41. Mongolia
9. Jordan	20. Kazakstan	31. Thailand	42. North Korea
10. Syria	21. Kyrgyzstan	32. Kampuchea	43. South Korea
11. Iraq	22. Tajikistan	33. Malaysia	44. Japan

Pacific Ocean

Indian Ocean

N
W E
S

0   2050 km

This map shows the countries of Asia. Some of these countries, such as Indonesia and the Philippines are made up of lots of islands. The people of Asia speak many different languages. In India there are sixteen **official** languages. But in western Asia most people speak the same language – Arabic.

Girl writing in school, China

Many Asian languages have their own alphabets that are used for writing. Some languages even have a different **symbol** for each word. Children in China have to learn thousands of symbols before they can read and write. Some Asian writing is read from right to left, and some from top to bottom.

Cities

Tokyo, Japan

Asia has some of the world's biggest cities. More people live in Tokyo than in any other city in the world. Tokyo is an important business centre with many modern skyscrapers. Bombay, in India, is another huge, crowded city. It was built on an island 700 years ago. Now, Bombay is famous for its film studios.

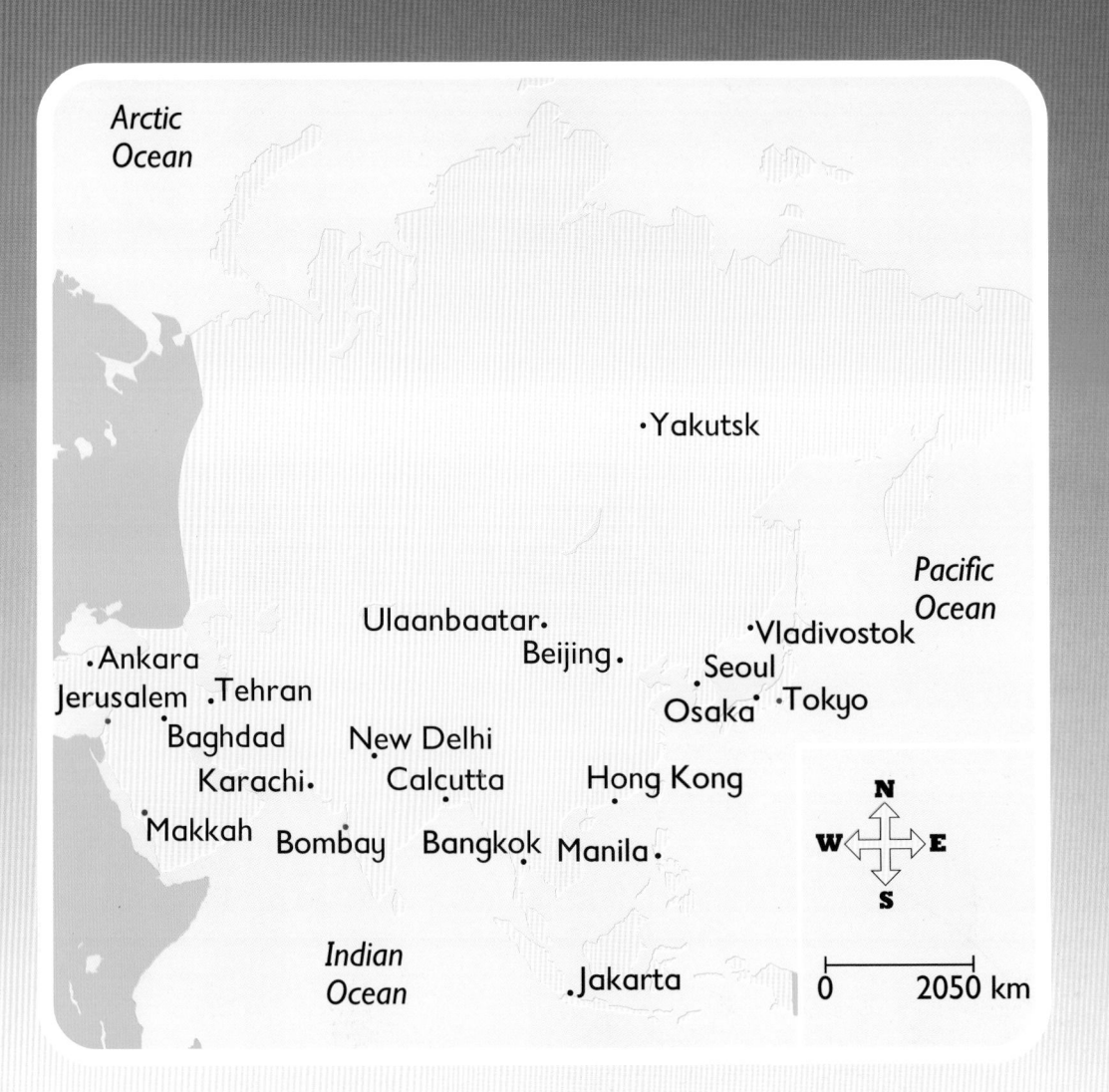

Arctic Ocean

·Yakutsk

Pacific Ocean

Ulaanbaatar·
Beijing·

·Vladivostok

·Ankara
Jerusalem ·Tehran
·Baghdad   New Delhi
Karachi·   Calcutta
·Makkah Bombay Bangkok Manila·

Seoul
Osaka· ·Tokyo

Hong Kong

N
W ⇦⇨ E
S

Indian Ocean

·Jakarta

0   2050 km

This map shows some of the most important cities in Asia.
Makkah, in Saudi Arabia, is the place where the **prophet
Muhammad** was born. **Muslims** from all over the world
try to visit Makkah at least once in their lifetime.
Wherever they are in the world, Muslims always pray
facing Makkah.

In the country

Bedouin camp, Pakistan

Wandering people, called Bedouins, live in the deserts of western Asia. The Bedouins sleep in tents and roam through the deserts, looking for places where their animals can feed. Bedouins often keep camels because these animals can survive for a long while without drinking water.

Floating market, Thailand

Many Asian farmers live in small villages close to their farms. They take their **crops** to markets, where they meet people from other villages and trade with them. Sometimes, farmers travel by boat to a floating market. People come to the banks of the river and buy food from the boats.

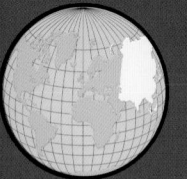 # Famous places

Great Wall of China

The Great Wall of China stretches across China for 6700 kilometres. It was built by the first emperor of China over 2000 years ago. The wall was meant to keep out fierce northern warriors. All along the wall are watchtowers where soldiers looked out for enemies. When they saw an enemy, they lit a fire in their tower.

Jerusalem, Israel

Jerusalem is a holy city for **Jews, Christians** and **Muslims**.
Inside the city is the Western Wall, part of a temple
built by a Jewish king over 2000 years ago. Jerusalem
also contains the Christian Church of the Holy Sepulchre,
and the Muslim Dome of the Rock.

Taj Mahal, India

The Taj Mahal is a beautiful **tomb** that a **Muslim** ruler, Shah Jahan, built for his wife, Mumtaz Mahal. The tomb is made from white marble and took 22 years to complete. Shah Jahan planned to build a matching tomb for himself out of black marble, but his son sent him to prison before building could start.

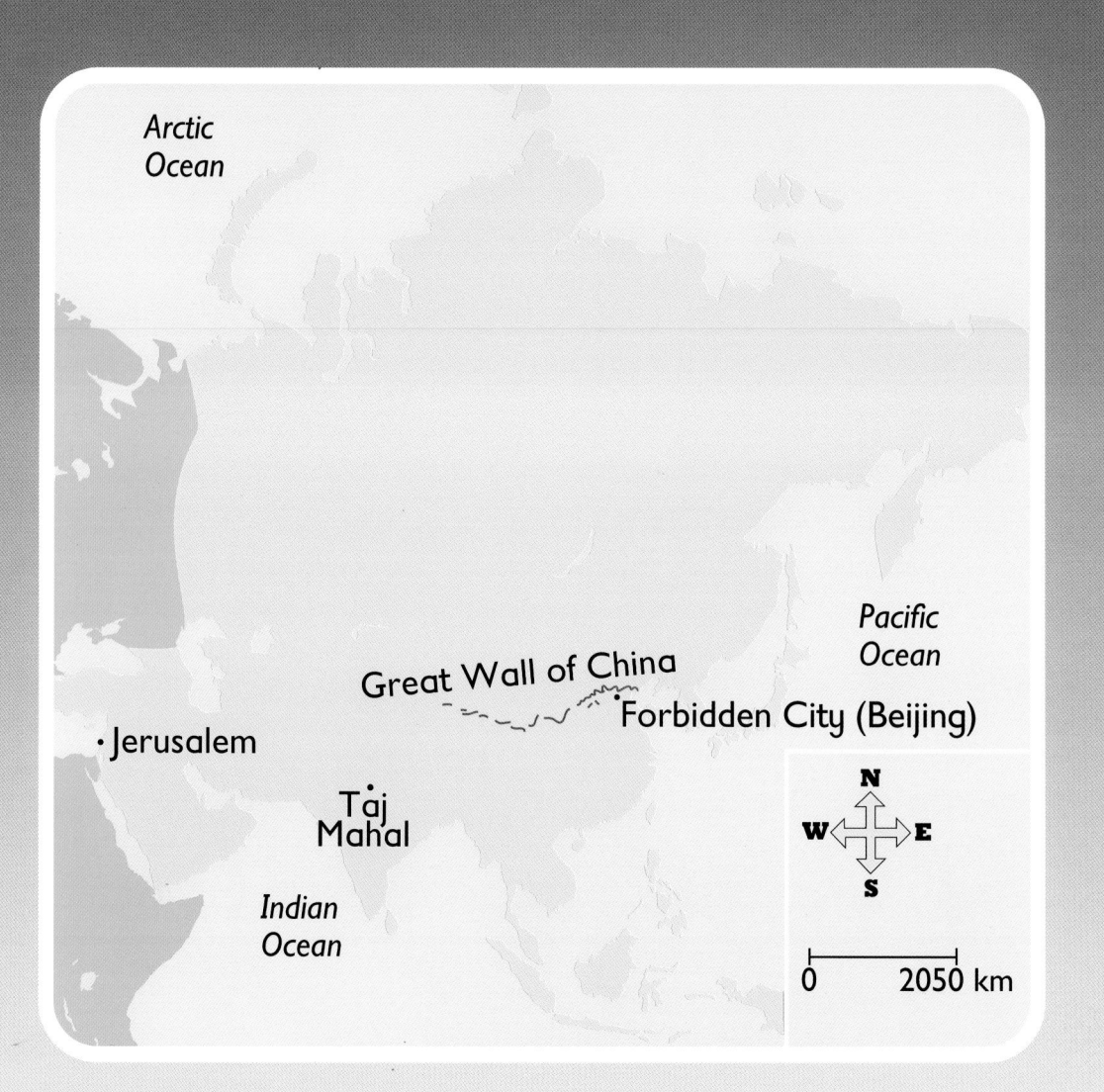

The Forbidden City is a huge walled palace inside the city of Beijing. It was built by Chinese emperors 600 years ago. Only the emperor's family and servants were allowed to enter the palace. For the next 500 years, the emperors lived inside the Forbidden City, completely cut off from their people.

Fast Facts

1. Over three billion people live in Asia – more than in any other continent.

2. Asia covers one third of all the land on Earth.

3. China has more people than any other country in the world. India has the second largest number of people.

4. The highest place on Earth, Mount Everest, is in Asia. It is 8850 metres tall.

5. Asia has the lowest place on Earth. The Dead Sea is 400 kilometres below sea level.

6. All the world's great religions started in Asia, including Judaism (the Jewish religion), Islam, Christianity, Buddhism and Hinduism.

7. Asia has the largest country in the world – Russia.

8. The Great Wall of China is the longest wall ever built. It is so large it can be seen from Space.

9. Asia is so huge that some places in the middle of the continent are more than 2500 kilometres from the sea.

Glossary

Arctic Circle imaginary line that circles the Earth near the North Pole

border dividing line between one country and another

Christian someone who follows the religion of Christianity, taught by Jesus Christ

climate kind of weather a place has

crop plant that is grown for food

equator imaginary circle around the exact middle of the Earth

export to send goods to another country to be sold

extinct no longer existing

fertile good for growing plants

humid hot and wet

Jew someone who follows the Jewish religion, based on the laws of Moses

mainland land that is part of a large country, rather than an island

mosque building used for worship by Muslims

Muhammad the founder of the religion of Islam

Muslim someone who follows the religion of Islam, taught by the prophet Mohammed

official approved by the government

prophet someone who tells about things that will happen in the future

rainforest thick forest that has heavy rain all the year round

range line of connected mountains

region large area, sometimes made up of several countries

saltwater water with salt in, like the sea

symbol something that represents another thing

tomb house or room where a dead person is buried

More books to read

Asia, Mike Graf, Bridgestone Books, 2002

An Illustrated Atlas of Asia, Keith Lye, Malcolm Porter, Cherrytree Books, 2000

Index